Please Don't Die

Amber Sweet-Davis

First paperback edition October 2025.

ISBN: 979-8-218-79797-3

ambersweetdavisauthor@gmail.com

Cover Art: Garth Morrissey
Author Photo: Samantha Covington
Editors: Kate Bassford-Baker and Stephanie Parent

For Parker.
Every word, every breath, every fight is for you.

PROLOGUE

The woman I was?

She believed in timing—
the right doors opening at the right moment.
I believe in tangled headphones and wine at noon.

She laughed easily—
full-bodied, head thrown back.
My laugh sounds like someone else's,
and I don't trust it.

She made plans months in advance—
detailed calendars and reservations.
I make plans in hours,
and even then, I half expect to cancel.

She cried at a swell of strings—
hands pressed against flushed cheeks.
I cry in bathrooms,
and resent the soundtrack of my own life.

She went out of her way to compliment strangers—
I barely look up, because small talk feels like a luxury.

She left every space better than she found it—
I'm just trying not to make a bigger mess.

She vanished the moment the world tilted.
I've made a life on shifting ground.

***

He changed—
not all at once.
Not in ways you'd notice right away.

I watched my child fade into a shell.
Sweating through his sickness.
Scan after scan.
Each one stripping something else away.

Then—
golden hair.

Now—
bare scalp,
strands abandoned on the pillow.

Then—
skin, soft and whole.

Now—
a port,
sitting in the cradle of a scar
that will outlive the sickness.

Then—
spoon to lips.

Crumbs. Laughter.

Now—a tube carries his meals,
where spoons rarely reach.

His body.
His boyhood.
Stolen.

We're ushered into the room.
Too cold. Too white.
The table—*wrong*.
Built for bad news.

Doctors.
Soft voices.
Eyes already sorry.
One asked if we want to see the scans.
"If you'd like…"

Like this is a tour.
Like we're choosing.
Like we could walk away.

And there it was—
Parker's tumor.

Lit up on the screen.
Bold. Brazen.
Like it wanted to be found.

The size of a walnut,
yet ruling the whole of him.

They said the word: *cancer*.
Calm. Practiced.
Someone slid a folder across the table.
I took it.
Because that's what you do.

You nod.
You receive.
You pretend you're still someone
who remembers how to sit in a chair.

That's when she cracked.
Not broken—ruptured.
Scattered.
Dust in hospital light.

I thought I'd already paid my dues.
My mother died when I was young.
That kind of grief
should count for something.
Like credit.
Or immunity.

I don't get a hall pass?

But grief doesn't care.
It doesn't calculate what you've endured.
It just comes back—
steady as a debt collector.

What came next
were the months that unmade me.

Ripped me down to bone.
Dragged me to the edge.
Told me to jump.

And I did.
Not from courage.
Not from choice.

But because
the ground behind me
was already gone.

CHAPTER 1

The whiteboard says Wednesday.
Feels like Tuesday.
Or last week.
Or the same day on repeat—
Groundhog Day,
but without Bill Murray to make it charming.

Everything split.
Time became something else.
A bruise we keep pressing.

The shock lives inside me
like a second heartbeat.
Heavy.
Endless.

I don't cry at the word anymore.
Don't flinch at the oncology sign.

Huh. That's new.

But I'm always bracing,
like something might drop from the ceiling,
the weight crushing what's left.

The rhythm here is relentless.

Intrusive. Unreasonable.
Vitals at midnight.
Again at four a.m.
The rip of Velcro before dawn.
IV pumps choking—
line full of air.
Nurses with soft voices
that somehow still feel like shouting.

I fold myself around him.

Careful.

Don't snag the lines.
Don't brush the feeding tube.

I don't remember what it's like to stretch out.
My back aches.
Joints click.

My body is giving itself away to keep him here.

Please don't die.

Rhythm.
Reflex.
Like blinking.
Like breathing.

I think it while I measure meds.
While I clean vomit from his mouth.
While I wipe his tears and say, "You're okay"—
when he's not,

and I'm not,
and none of this is.

I nod through lab results.

Ahh yes. Numbers. Of course.

Could've been Morse code.
IKEA instructions.
At least those have diagrams
and a false sense of control.

I count time in units of suffering now.

Treatment cycles.
Procedures.
Clinic appointments.

The number of times
we've pinned him down
and called it mercy—
like rebranding pain makes it better.

Parker sleeps.
I scroll.
Looking for something to hate.
Writing texts I forget to send.

Michael brings food.
Cold sushi from the cafeteria.
I eat. I drink. I fade.

Wander the halls.

Wash the clothes.
One laundry room for the whole floor.
As if life wasn't cruel enough.

Step in the elevator—perfume.
Sweet. Floral. Pretty.
I hate it instantly.
Not for the scent itself—because it doesn't belong here.

It smells of a world
that still gets to pretend.

Then—back.
A rash. A number.
A doctor using *the voice*.

Life, reduced to pins and needles.

You learn to read the silences.
The pause before they ask you to step out.
The way they say your name.
The tilt of pity.
The squint.

I thank the nurses for more towels.
Force myself under hot water—
scrub the sadness until I'm raw.
I spread retinol all over my face,
like I believe wrinkles are the problem.

"We're fine," I say, when we're not.
Because if I let the truth all the way in,
I might not make it back.

Please don't take him.

I've always been good at the cover.
Earned my badge early—
four years old,
walking back into the world
after the crash that took my mother.

Smile. Nod.
Don't let them see me fall apart.
Just enough scaffolding
to keep me upright
while everything underneath gives way.

I was so good at structure.
Admired for it, even.
Routines. Clean edges.
The quiet sort of discipline
that holds a household together.

Now—there's no plan.
I can't fix this.
Can't mother it into submission.
Can't love the cancer out of him.

All I can do is stay.
Hold him through the pain.
Find words when he asks,
"Mommy, what are they going to do to me today?"

Watching—
to see if I'll tell him the truth.

I used to think in seasons. In years. In plans.

Now—hours. Sometimes minutes.

This isn't a crisis.
This is the long haul.

The part where you stop checking for exits
because you live here now.

Please don't die.

Please.

Don't—

The only prayer I have left.

This isn't a detour.
This is the road.

CHAPTER 2

His preschool teachers waved me over on the playground.
"He just seems…sadder somehow," they said.
"We can't quite explain it."

I could.

It was already starting to show itself—
small and sly.

That tiny hitch in his step,
gone almost as soon as it came.

Not enough to panic.
Just enough to catch in my spine
before my eyes had time to agree.

I didn't know what I was looking at.
But it lodged in me anyway.

That's how it started.
A soft drag of one foot.
The kind of thing you notice
and tell yourself not to overthink.

But then you keep seeing it.
Quietly.

Repeatedly.
Like a hairline crack in the glass—
warning you the whole pane is about to shatter.

Night sweats.
Hair slick to his forehead.
Sheets tangled like seaweed.
He blinked at me—confused,
no fever, no cough.
Only a small, startled boy in the dark.

They said it was probably post-viral.
"Kids get weird symptoms," they said.

How reassuring.

Fatigue.
Not tantrums.
Not crankiness.
A slow retreat.

My bright, curious boy began to fade.
He wanted to lie down in the middle of the day.
Ignored his toys.
Stopped asking why things worked.
Curled into blankets and stared at the screen.

Gone, in some way I couldn't name.
A weight in his eyes.
An old grief wearing a new, small body.

That's when the panic began to hum.

***

We were moving.
Just bought our first house.
Boxes half-packed.
Movers to hire.
A closet full of untouched things.
Too much noise.

The kind you can hide inside
if you want to pretend nothing's wrong.

My son—
breaking open in ways
I couldn't see clearly.
Not because I looked away—
because I didn't know better.

Another waiting room.
More scans.

The ER doctor said transient synovitis.
Common.
Rest. Fluids. Ibuprofen.
Give it time.

Michael and I clung to that certainty like a raft.
One we didn't notice was already leaking.

But the limp got worse.
His spark was gone.
I stopped sleeping.

Another specialist.
Another layer of dread.

Parker sat beside me, legs dangling,
playing a game on my phone.

And I heard it louder this time—
Something is wrong.

The orthopedist asked about his weight loss.
Two pounds in two weeks.

Her brow furrowed.
My heart dropped.

Then she looked at me—
not as a doctor, but as a mother.
"Mom to mom," she said.
"Go to the ER. Now. I'll call ahead."

That was it.
The ground tilted.

She didn't say cancer.
Maybe she couldn't.

Women know.
Even when we beg for doubt,
our skin still feels it.
The body never whispers by accident.

I nodded.
Thanked her.

Carried Parker out in silence.
I drove straight to the city.
Told Michael to meet me there.
Called my best friend, Samantha—
she was on her way before I put the phone down.

***

The ER was chaos.
Fluorescents.
X-rays.
Bloodwork.
Questions that made my stomach twist.

They didn't send us home.
That was the first real sign.

Five days of hell.

Watching him vanish beneath the sheets.
Hushed voices behind the curtain.
Pain clawing through his body.
And us—unraveling, thread by thread.

The guilt bloomed.
Because I knew.

Even as I folded tiny socks into boxes.
Even as I highlighted the inspection report.
While we were taping up to-do lists,
chasing the future—our son was slipping away.

That doctor didn't warn me.
She confirmed what I already knew.

I wasn't crazy.
I wasn't paranoid.

That night, while Parker slept—
wrapped in his dinosaur blanket,
the only familiar thing in the room—
I sat in the dark and said it.

Not a thought.
Not an idea
I was trying on for size.
A prayer.

Please don't die.

I didn't know it was cancer.
But I heard something fracture in the air between us.
Time split clean down the center.

Before. And after.

CHAPTER 3

Dr. Squints-a-Lot asked us to *step out*.
Always a good sign.

Separate room. A folder.
Box of tissues.
The script doesn't just write itself—
it's been workshopped a thousand times.

Parker stayed behind with two nurses,
eating an electric-blue popsicle—
a gift from the attending.

Her squint of pity
said everything
her mouth refused to say.

Michael sat beside me.
Samantha next to him—steady.
She had been there since day one.
She opened a notebook
and clicked her pen without a word.

Three doctors. One nurse practitioner.
One held a folder.
Another, a stack of papers.
All of them wearing the same expression—

composed, rehearsed, bracing.

The fellow spoke gently.
"We found a mass," he said.

Oh. The mass you already told us was nothing?

My stomach clenched, hot with rage.

He kept going:
"It's wrapped around the adrenal gland.
Based on imaging and labs,
we believe it's neuroblastoma."

Neuroblastoma.
I'd never heard the word before.
But my body knew.
The syllables dropped like iron into my chest.

"High risk."
"Chemotherapy."
"Two years."

Michael and I locked eyes.
We knew—our old life was over.
There was no way back.

Samantha took notes—fast, calm, unwavering.
The only one not frozen.

Michael sat with fists on his knees, knuckles white—
like if he moved,
everything would splinter.

How long had it been growing?

How long had it been stealing from him—and we didn't know?

How many nights did I kiss his forehead and miss the war beneath?

As if the room heard me…

"You did nothing wrong," one of them said.
"There's nothing you could have done."
"It's just… bad luck."

Bad luck.
Fuck you.

As if cancer is a raffle.
Like our number just came up.

Rage: doubled.

It echoed through me: *Your son has cancer.*

And beneath that, louder: *Your son might die.*

I wasn't breathing.
I was hovering—split from myself,
suspended in a moment too big to hold.

They said more words:
"Protocol."
"Outcomes."
"Survival rates."

The fellow even drew a chart—
lines, arrows,
hope-shaped scribbles.
None of it mattered.
This wasn't a conversation.

It was a sentence.

The clock shattered mid-tick,
then lurched forward—
into a time I didn't recognize.

Eventually, we stood.
Michael nodded like he was listening.
Samantha closed her notebook slowly.
We followed the doctors out like ghosts
who hadn't realized they were dead yet.

And there he was.
Parker.
My sweet boy.
Sitting upright in his hospital bed.
Popsicle in hand.

Blue mouth.
Blue tongue.
Blue joy.

"Mama," he said. "It's blue!"

I said something back.
I smiled.

I made my face do the right thing.

Because he didn't know yet.
He was still inside the *Before*.

The sun still shone through the window.
The machines still hummed.
But everything had changed.

Neuroblastoma didn't just name the thing inside his body.
It burned down the life we knew.

The terror didn't start in that cold room.
It started after—
the moment I had to walk back in and be his mother,
pretending I hadn't just watched our future go up in flames.

The air was smoke.
It filled my lungs.
It stole my life.

I haven't breathed the same way since.

CHAPTER 4

The boy I knew is blurring into someone else.
I miss him.

Sprinting down hallways.
Racing us to the door.
Ukulele in his hands—
strumming like the world was leaning in.

Dancing without music.
Joy in every limb.
Gummies by the fistful.
Strawberries until his arms were sticky—
freedom staining his skin.

Who knew freedom was organic?

Sometimes the past hurts more than now—
because it's the version of him
the world will never see again.

Sweet baby breath.
Foot resting on the highchair tray.
His weight in my arms.
Heavy with trust.

He still exists.

I see him—sudden, bright.
Laughing at his own punchlines
like they're the first joke he ever told.

For a second—I remember.
For a second—I forget.

A flicker
fast enough to make me doubt I saw it.

Then the hospital calls.
We hand him over.
The *Before* version
still warm in my hands.

Back to advocating.
Back to being complicit.

***

He rages now.
It's the meds, the pain, the trauma—
no one can separate them cleanly.

He's angry in ways that don't belong to him.
I see it boil behind his eyes.
The way he throws things.
Hits. Screams.

Says things he doesn't mean—
just to see if the room will recoil.

I just sit there.
Let it stay broken.

He battles the body that betrayed him.
Fights to hold what's still his.

Glazed eyes.
Pain filling the room.
The flicker fades.

A ghost—
still wanting French fries.
Screen time.

Falls asleep mid-episode.
Slime hugged to his chest.
Cars lined up like they've sworn an oath.

No one tells you about that grief.
The kind that starts before the loss.
The kind that haunts the living.

He was color.
Noise.
Light.
Now—pale.
Tubes and scars.
Hooked to poison meant to save him.

The dark lingers in the doorway.
Hungry.
Tries to swallow him whole.

Back. Off.

Too much of him.
Too much fight.
Too much love
for it to get the last bite.

Even as I watch him—
I miss him.

Until then—
I'll take him like this:
iPad clutched like it holds the last good thing,
dog video on loop,
laughing—
just to spite the dark.

CHAPTER 5

At some point, I stopped crying.
The grief calcified.
Hardened into routine.

I don't remember when—
only that one day, the tears dried up.

What was left wasn't peace or strength.
It was emptiness.

A strange, weightless quiet.
Like someone turned down the volume on my life.
And I forgot how to turn it back up.

Still here.

People think grief looks like screaming.
Sometimes it does.
I have.

I have cried so hard I couldn't breathe—
curled up in the hospital shower, shaking.
Pleading with the air not to take my child.

But that kind of grief burns hot. Fast.
You can't survive it for long.

Still breathing.

Now I move through the days outside my body.
Watching from a few seconds behind.
Like someone else is wearing me.
I could rent my body out to another mom entirely—
one who knows the schedule.

Daily injections.
Tube feeds.
Did we refill the antibiotic?
More barf bags in the diaper bag.

Nothing says childhood like colorful vomit vessels.

I sign consent forms.
I ask questions—
in a voice that sounds calm.
Professional, even.
But I am not calm.
I'm numb.

And numbness lets me function.
And function is how we survive.

Still moving.

I used to think numbness was weakness.
Now I know—
It's armor.
A mercy.
The body's shutdown switch.

Somewhere inside, my brain decided:
You can't feel all of this.
I'll carry what I can.

But every now and then—
something cuts through.
Sharp enough to prove I'm still here.

Like when Parker vomits for the third time in an hour.
I'm holding the bag, rubbing his back.
Whispering, "You're doing so good, baby."

And he snaps:
"Don't say that."

I know that tone.
It's not anger.
It's edge.

Exhaustion.
Truth.

What he means is:
Don't lie to me.
Don't cheer for this.

He's tired.
It hurts.
It's too much for a small body to carry.

People call him resilient.
Tough.

Amazing.

They don't see that shift.
The hardening—
softness learning self-defense.

Not to impress.
Not to perform.

He's fighting to stay himself.

To hold on to whatever pieces of his childhood
haven't been taken yet.

Some days, that fight
looks like telling us to leave.
Refusing our praise.
Glaring at me
when I try to cheer him up
with too much light.

So we walk the halls
while he stays behind with his Nanny.

Swallow the urge to fix.
But inside—it shatters me.
Because comfort used to be easy.

Now I'm not sure what helps.
Love feels like overstepping.

Letting him push me away
might be the most brutal kind of love

I've ever had to give.

And still—I rarely cry.
Because numb is safer.

Numb lets me say,
"Platelets are low," and
"We got into the study,"
without shaking.

Numb lets me smile
when someone says,
"You're so strong,"
without wanting to scream.

I'm not strong.

I'm surviving.

That's different.

Sometimes survival
looks like showing up
without feeling a damn thing.

Like holding your child
while your heart goes quiet.

Because broken
means collapse.

But numb—
numb means you're still standing.

Even if you're not sure why.

CHAPTER 6

I thought this was our first trauma.
But Parker's diagnosis cracked something older—
a fault line I didn't know was still alive.

And something in me snapped.
Not just from fear—
but from memory.

Four.
My mother died in a car crash I survived.

Four.
They said the word that threatened to take my son.

Four and four.
Symmetry like a curse.

Flashbacks—
burning rubber,
silence,
wind.

That bone-deep knowing
something is terribly wrong
before anyone
dares say it out loud.

Now it lives in hospitals—
in the breath before results,
the pause before a doctor speaks,
the godforsaken squint.

I wonder if they teach that in med school.

Trauma doesn't vanish.
It waits in the body—
polite until it isn't.

When your child is four,
and you were four—
it rushes in.
Too fast.

Like a tide,
dragging both of you under at once.

Suddenly I'm not just a mother holding her son.
I'm a daughter losing her mother.

The little girl—seatbelt loose, legs swinging,
trying to wake someone who won't wake up.

The woman—beside her son in a hospital bed,
begging the world not to do it again.

I think of my dad—
brushing my hair,
frying my bologna,
saying, "It's going to be okay,"

with a voice that didn't believe it.

He couldn't bear to talk about her.
Or maybe my stepmom wouldn't let him.
Either way, the silence was devastating.

He carried his grief like a secret—
buried deep, sealed tight,
but shaping every room he entered.

Broken, but still moving.

We are living the same life.
Parenting in the undertow—
keeping them afloat
while something unseen
pulls at your feet.

***

I wonder how he told us.

How do you tell two children
their mother is gone?

Where did he sit?
What words did he choose?
I don't remember.

Only the air—
thick, certain—
that nothing

would ever be the same.

And then I'm here.
Across from Parker.
Michael beside me.

Telling our son he has cancer.
Soft words.
Gentle ones.

You're safe.
We love you.

What was he thinking?
Was he scared?
Did the world fracture for him, the way it did for me?

I wanted to protect him.
My baby.
The way my dad wanted to protect me.
Some words take everything.
It doesn't matter how you say them.

I didn't just lose my mom.
I lost the version of me
who believed tragedy only strikes once.

No one told me
you can lose the same thing
again and again.

Please don't die.

I am a mother
trying to save her son.

A daughter
still aching for her mother.

A four-year-old again—
begging the world
not to take her person.

CHAPTER 7

I stalk the hallway.
Trying to shake the quiet off my back.

It's there—breathing.
Waiting to pounce. Like it knows
I'm about to break.

Asshole.

A call nurse steps in front of me.
Takes my hands.
"Can I pray with you?"

Like she's offering a snack I didn't ask for.

I nod.
Too stunned to pull away.
Pinned by kindness that feels like a trap.

Her prayers land like a trespass—
breaking in where they don't belong.

Oh good, rage again.

Your holy words are for you—
a lullaby to quiet the part of you

that can't bear my pain.

Stop trying to make suffering beautiful.

This is not a battle.
Not a journey.
Not a test from the sky.

It's the slow dismantling of my child—
and me, imploding quietly enough
that he can't hear the fracture.

Parker just wants his body back.
To go home.
To be a kid.

He's four.

Believes in magic. Plays with dinosaurs. Digs for boogers.

People call him strong
because they need him to be.

But I see a boy's spirit push through—
not for applause.
Not for anyone.

Because just being Parker
is the last thing cancer hasn't stolen.

That's not strength.
That's survival.

***

When my mom died,
people told me I was "brave."

Told my dad he was "so strong"—
for showing up at school functions,
for keeping his collapse out of sight.

But I saw it—
even when others looked away.

Re-married quickly, not for love, but survival.

A woman he'd grow to loathe—
just so we could call her "mom."

Let her wipe my mother's memory clean.

He never went to the grave.
He packed away the photos.
He barely whispered her name.

Chose the barstool, the dark.
Because it was easier
than what waited at home.

Wore his heartbreak
like a weighted vest,
tightening with every step.

Too heavy to take off.
Too familiar to set down.

Maybe it was the only way he could keep breathing.

And I wasn't brave.
I was four.
Too young to choose anything.

Resilience was *issued* to us—
a fucking badge I'd burn if I could.

Now they're pinning it on Parker.
On me.
On Michael.

Calling us strong
so they can stay at a safe distance
and still feel good.

I hate being strong.
I reject it.

It's just suffering with better posture.
Pain with contour and concealer.

If you want to help—
don't hand me hope wrapped in denial.

Sit with me in the dark.

We'll get there—
if we get there—
but only by telling the truth.

CHAPTER 8

They update the whiteboard.
Or they don't.
The same nurse's name lingers for days,
like time gave up and nobody noticed.

They say healing happens here.
Feels more like suffering dressed in protocol.
Pain measured in numbers.
Silence where facts belong.

The hospital vortex.

We hate it in our bones.
In our spines,
bruised by cots more spring than mattress.
In our eyes,
burned by lights that never dim.
In our nerves,
frayed by alarms that shriek at three a.m.—
and again at noon.

God forbid we forget where we are.

Clockwork cruelty.

Time folds in on itself.

Days collapse into moments.
Moments stretch into weeks.
We've been here forever.
Or maybe just a minute.

Does it even matter?

The food isn't even bad.
Which somehow feels worse.
We eat—
salt seeping into our veins,
marinating us in grief.

The machines never miss a beat.
Unbothered.
Mechanical.
Their rhythm dares ours to falter.

And they give me a fucking eye twitch.

Michael and I orbit each other— half-awake,
exhaustion like a second skin.
Pajamas on.
Doors opening.
Buttons pressed.
Tissues restocked.

Go away.

Breathe.
Don't give it to them here.
Not where they'll file it away.
Keep it for the silence

that belongs only to you.

Scaffolding.
Thin, borrowed strength.
Just enough to keep from caving.

I sleep beside Parker every night,
both of us clenched,
holding fear like it might spill—
and if it does,
it will crawl into every corner
and write the ending for us.

Some days I don't leave the room.
The walls blur.
I forget the sky exists.

When I do escape—
it's like falling out of orbit.
Sun hotter than I remember,
streets thick with errands,
faces set to rhythm.

I walk among them,
but I'm not really there.
Just another body, out of sync.

The world hums along, unmarked.
But we stay.
Because this place holds the medicine.
The research.

The only shot we have.

It pretends to love him.
Pretends he's more than a number.
But it doesn't love him.
It doesn't love us.

It trades in scans and blood counts.
Offers life through a needle.
Takes pieces of him in return.

This place is our lifeline.
And our captor.

***

Parker knows the protocol.
Turns toward the nurse.
Lifts his arm.
Stillness.
The Velcro bites into his skin.
Her eyes barely meet mine.
For her, routine.
For us, the whole damn day.

He calls his feeding tube his "tubi."
When they placed it,
I thought it might break me.
Another thing sticking out of him.

Defiance and exhaustion,
sharing the same body.
Small, and ancient, in the same breath.

His bald head—
even now—
still startles me.
Undeniable.
Proof the old life is gone.

He adjusted before Michael and me.
Let his hair fall out—refused to shave it.
Pushes the meds himself.
Knows the syringes.
Knows what they do.

He's four.
And even here,
in the heart of the vortex,
fear bends to him.

***

We were home, between rounds.
That strange, suspended stretch—
the worst had passed for now,
but the next hit was already scheduled.

No pumps. No nurses.
Just the fridge humming
like it didn't get the memo.

Parker asleep on the couch,
curled in his dinosaur blanket,
cheeks round and pink with sleep.

Breathing soft.
Unfighting.

I sat near him,
pretending to do anything but wait.

Then the light shifted—
sunlight spilling across the living room,
catching his skin just right.

For one impossible second,
he looked untouched.
Like nothing had ever happened.

Glowing—
like the boy I've been chasing through memory.

Like the *Before* was still reachable,
if only for a breath.

Maybe if I stay still—
if I just don't move, we can stay here.

Just him.
Just light.
Just a moment that doesn't hurt.

But the light shifted.
The spell broke.

And the countdown started again—
the clock in the corner smirking like it knows.

***

The storm always comes back.
It finds us every time.

But it's not the same Parker who meets it.
It's the one carved by procedures and pauses.
The one who's learned to listen
for what isn't said.

When the doctors walk in, he doesn't smile.
He just asks, flat and certain,
"What are you going to do to me?"

Because he already knows.

He stays braced—
for pain, for the next needle,
for the small invasions dressed up as care.

He looks at me, already knowing what's next.
I climb onto the bed, pull him close.
Whisper, "Just one more poke."

He thrashes.
Screams, "No thank you!"
Begs us to stop.

We don't.
We can't.

This is love now—
quicksand disguised as parenting.

We hate the vortex.
But we stay.

Because this place might save him.
And that has to be enough.

The whiteboard still says Wednesday.

CHAPTER 9

Parker swipes his line of cars aside—
neat, perfect, now forgotten.

The doll lies on the tray table.
He wipes the chest with an alcohol swab.
"Cold and wet," he whispers—
the same quiet warning they use.

They call it medical play.
But there's nothing playful
about the way he lines up his supplies—
syringes, IV butterflies, grip locks.

He narrates everything, just like they do:
"Okay, I'm going to clean your port now."
"This medicine helps your body get strong."
"We have to do some hard things."

Not pretend—repair.

Tenderness for the part of himself still hurting.
Meaning where fear used to live.

Michael and I watch from the couch.
Afraid to move.
Afraid to disturb

this sacred reassembling.

He's absorbed it all—
the cadence,
the careful words adults use
when they're about to hurt you.

And somehow,
instead of collapsing under it,
he's turned it into understanding.
Agency. Mastery.

Fear yields to him.

He watches videos now—
not just *Paw Patrol,*
but "Why do we get shots?"
"What is surgery?"
"How does anesthesia work?"

Not exactly the bedtime playlist I pictured.

He doesn't flinch.
Not because he isn't scared—
but because he has been scared, and he came through.

Maybe for him, survival begins with naming—
mapping every corner before it closes in.

He's shown us resilience has nothing to do with strength—
and everything to do with refusing
to let the world unmake you.

He fights to be Parker.
That's the miracle.

Even inside pain,
he insists on choice—
even if it's just who holds the syringe.

We're supposed to be his protectors.
Most days—it's the other way around.
We scramble to keep pace with him.

When the dark taunts from the doorway,
when we forget what hope feels like, he reminds us:
Survival isn't a story, isn't a performance.

It's a child—steady-handed,
holding a syringe,
saying, *"Okay. I'm ready."*

Daring the dark to try again.

CHAPTER 10

Sometimes his face fools me—
pink-cheeked, eyes wide,
breath steady, centered.

Eating cheese puffs
like it's a race, five in a row,
orange dust coating his fingers.

If you didn't know, you wouldn't.
Just a kid in the middle of a good day.

Climbs into my lap,
all carbs and trust,
and for a moment,
I almost believe the lie.

He folds into me—
small, yet heavy,
weight that doesn't match his size.

Like he's trying to go back.
Back to when safety still felt possible.

Blue eyes—
clear, unguarded.
One more book.

The scrape of the stepstool.
Me at the stove.

I hold him tighter,
like maybe I can keep us there.

***

Room 18, South Tower.
The most coveted corner of the oncology floor.

Far enough from the ER
to escape the screams.
Close enough to the laundry
to pretend clean clothes mean control.

Parker's eyes are half-closed.
Voice soft.

"Twinkle Twinkle Little Star."
The Jewel version. On repeat.

Bedtime, back when bedtime was just bedtime.

I play it.
The song pulls him under.
Breath catches. Softens. Drifts.

I break.
No tears. No sound.
Just shatter from the inside out.

The *Before* flashes—blinding.

Soft pajamas.
Polka-dot sheets.
The blue nightlight glow.
The ordinary.

Michael steps in from the family lounge,
arms full of vending machine snacks.
He stops cold.
Sees me shaking over Parker's body.

No words.
No questions.
Everything drops.
Snacks scatter.

Then he's around me—
chest a wall, arms a barricade,
like if he could just hold me tightly enough,
neither of us would shatter.

The song winds around us both.
I feel it find him—
threading through his chest,
dragging him into the same memory that's breaking me.

We sink together.
Under the weight of the music.
The memory.
The fear we'll never get him back.

Not the way he was—
not without parts carved out.

Of him. Of us.

CHAPTER 11

Two weeks off between cycles.
Off—like cancer takes PTO.

Seven days wrecked:
poison burning through,
vomit on demand,
shrinking inside his clothes,
house sealed tight.

Seven days waiting for the wreck to return:
counting every calorie,
stepping outside again,
pretending at normal—
knowing it won't last.

Friends bring soup.
"He looks amazing," they say—
but they don't smell the vomit,
don't hear the pump at night,
don't see him thrash.

I miss my old life.
Chaos mornings.
Errands stacked.
Arguing with myself in the grocery aisle—
oat or almond,

as if it meant anything.

Once in Target,
Parker begged for a toy piano we already owned.
I said no.
He collapsed—
as if I'd canceled Christmas and oxygen.

How dare I.

Back then, failure.
Now, a miracle.

***

After round one,
we came home carrying a hospital.
Bedroom turned storage.
Clorox. Gloves. Masks.
Feeding bags stacked high.
A house built for survival, not living.

The waiting room
isn't a hallway anymore.
It's everywhere.

Not a home—
but the *Before*,
frozen mid-sentence.

Sometimes I walk through it
like a museum of ruins:

"Here's where we were going to be happy."
"Here's where everything stopped."

We all sleep in the same bed now.
At first, he wouldn't even go into his room—
too quiet, too far.
So we pulled him in.

He's always between us.
Our tether.
His small body anchoring ours,
so none of us drift too far in our dreams.

I need that too.
Every cough knots my chest.
Every "Mommy, I need you"
pulls me up from whatever
half-sleep I've managed.

Push the meds.
Flush the line.
Scrub the syringes.
Barf bags live in every room.
Dinosaur print—Amazon's idea of comfort.
Some nights, I fall asleep holding one.

I sleep in half-states,
curled around him like a parenthesis—
eyes closed, ears alert.

Sometimes Parker shifts
and I sit up—summoned.
He coughs, and I'm reaching

before I think.

Calm isn't safe.
It's the setup.

Always ready.
No manual.
Count breaths.
Sniff for infection.
Repeat.

Try to read a book.
Plots vanish. Words dissolve.
Even scrolling, I'm braced.
Wired. Waiting.
No off switch.

Parker sleeps—beautifully, honestly.
He's earned the peace
that keeps skipping over Michael and me.

They call it caregiver fatigue,
as if we just need a *nap*.

Michael sleeps in bursts.
Ready, but not like me.
Not tuned to every twitch
like it might be the start—
or the end.

Sometimes I envy him.
Sometimes I resent him.
Mostly, I miss him.

Even when he's right there. Silent.
Screens glowing.
Touching without touching.

Survival leaves little room for softness.
Even love feels rationed.

Tomorrow I'll try to reach for him.
If there's anything left of me to reach.

I won't shut down.
Not now.
Not while there's so much to fight for.

CHAPTER 12

Someone's in my kitchen.
Or texting.
Or FaceTiming.

Reaching out in all the ways people do now.
Just enough to stay close.
Not enough to unravel.

It's always the same.
They start to vent—
about work, their kid, their body.
Something ordinary.
Something human.

Then they pause.
Catch themselves.
"Ugh, sorry. It's not a big deal.
Not like what you're going through."

It happens a lot.
People edit themselves around me.
Like I've become the benchmark for pain.

But hard is relative.
You don't need cancer to feel like you're falling apart.
There are no Grief Olympics.

Oh my god, can you even imagine?

Don't disqualify your suffering
just because mine has a name and a treatment plan.

***

I remember the early days of motherhood,
lost in the fog of postpartum.

Hemorrhoids.
Sore nipples.
Crippling anxiety.

"We have notes." - Mothers everywhere.

Trying to find rhythm in a life I chose but didn't yet recognize.

Two years of nursing.
Never off the clock.
My whole identity stripped down
to feedings, naps, stroller loops.

I had chosen it.
Dreamed of it.
Left a career I loved.
Built this life on purpose.

And still—
I felt empty sometimes.
Lonely in a house filled with love.

So grateful I ached.
So isolated I wanted to scream.

Madly in love with motherhood.
Still longing for the version of me I set down.

Two things can be true.

So when someone says,
"I didn't want to bother you with my stuff,"
or
"It just felt silly compared to what you're going through"—
I want to shake them.

Gently.

Then say:
Don't do that.

Don't tuck your truth behind mine
like it doesn't count.
Because it does.
I want to hear your hard.

You can be devastated for me
and still gutted by your own life.

You can be afraid for my son
and still drowning
in your own exhaustion.

You can cry for me and cry for yourself.

Both matter.

We all carry weight.
We all break under different loads.

Say the thing.
Even if it's small.
Even if it's nothing next to cancer.

I can hold both.
So can you.

That's how we carry each other home.

CHAPTER 13

No one tells you how isolation can bloom right next to love.
How grief rearranges even the way two bodies share a mattress.

We lie beside each other in the dark.
Same bed. Same breath.
His hand on one side of Parker.
Mine on the other.

And still, some nights, we're oceans apart—
in the same storm,
each tied to our own sinking.

The *Cancer Binder* didn't cover this part.
Plenty about feeding tubes and mouth sores.
No chapter about the slow erosion of intimacy.
Nothing about holding each other like strangers
because you're too tired to speak.

No tab for *How to Stay Human While Your Life Burns Down.*
I guess we're supposed to figure that one out ourselves.

I love that for us.

They never tell you how love can sit quietly between two people—
wordless, worn out, and aching for something to say.

Michael and I are in this together.
Every decision.
Every scan.
Every low-voiced meeting
outside his door.

But grief doesn't move in sync.

Sometimes he cries when I can't.
Sometimes I rage when he shuts down.
Sometimes we sit side by side
and feel a thousand miles apart.

Pretending the distance isn't growing.
Pretending the silence is just fatigue.
But the cost of that quiet is enormous.

Everyone thinks we're doing great.
Really it's just two of us—
bracing against the corners,
hoping the whole thing holds.

I see his grief in his grip on the chair.
Eyes fixed on Parker's face—
like love might undo the nightmare.
In the way he keeps asking questions—
not because he doesn't understand,
but because he needs something solid to hold.

I wonder how he sees my grief.
If he mistakes it for anger.
If he confuses it for distance.
If he even sees it at all.

PLEASE DON'T DIE

Where is the manual for staying married while your child might die?

We try.
Whisper I love you across IV lines.
Hold hands in hallways.
Melt into each other—
more exhausted than connected.

The space between us
feels like another diagnosis.

***

Parker kicked Michael out.
Screamed it from the hospital bed. "Leave."
Four years old, and he meant it.

Michael walked out with the blame.
I stayed with the boy who had sent him away.

Hours later, I woke to find him back—
eyes locked on our son's face
like he could will something into being.

He wasn't crying.
He was unraveling.
Silently. Devastatingly.
Hand hovering inches above Parker's blanket,
like it might undo the pain.

His love was loud in the quiet.

So loud it crushed me.

He didn't look at me.
Didn't speak.

Just stared,
like he was memorizing Parker's face—
in case he ever had to recreate it from memory.

The next morning,
he handed me coffee.
Sat beside me.
We watched Parker sleep.
Together this time.

And I reached for his hand.
Not because anything had been fixed.
Not because we were okay.
But because that's what you do
when your person is breaking
and you are too.
You reach.
And you stay.

Sometimes I want to fall apart in his arms.
I can tell he needs the same.
But we don't let ourselves.
Not because we don't love each other—
but because the weight is too delicate.
If one of us crumbles, what happens to Parker?

***

I remember our old nightly ritual.
Exhausted from the bedtime gauntlet.
Everything quiet.

Michael and I on the couch,
sharing popcorn and wine.
Watching our favorite show.
Laughing at the same line before it even happened.
Not talking about anything heavy—just close.
Tired.
Happy.
Ordinary.

Those nights were glue.
They built something we'd later need to survive on.

Now we sleep with Parker in our bed.
His little hand reaching for us.
That tether we all need.
A reminder: we're still here.

Still trying to find each other
in the storm that hasn't passed.

We don't always touch. But we reach.
We don't always speak. But we stay.

Maybe that's what our love looks like now:
Not easy.
Not romantic.
But loyal.
Brutal.
Present.

We are trying to hold him.

Trying to hold us.
Trying to hold on.

CHAPTER 14

Rage was missing from the pamphlet.
Easier to talk tumors than tempers.

They hand you the pep talks instead:
Fertility loss.
Weight loss.
Hearing loss.

So much loss.

No one warns you that a photo of a kid eating birthday cake
might make you want to smash a plate.

Or that you might fantasize about hurling a chair across the room
just to hear something break the way you have.

I am furious.
Quietly.
Loudly.
Constantly.

Furious at cancer, obviously—
The monster that crawled into my child's body
and started stealing from him.

Please don't die.

But it's not just cancer.

I'm mad at the hospital—
its forced cheer,
its stupid bright colors.

Mad at the oncology floor,
where the lights are too bright
and the noises never stop.

Mad at the staff who slip you a meal voucher—
like they see us eating our feelings
and mistake it for hunger.

Mad at the doctors
who make mistakes like they're allowed to learn on the job.

Mad at the ones who squint before saying something awful—
like maybe the squint will soften the blow.

I hate their fucking squint.

I'm mad at the nurses who say,
"You're doing great,"
while pinning my screaming child down.

Mad that we still have to ask about parking validation
while our son might be dying.

Mad at the friends who disappeared.
Mad at the ones who stayed and said all the wrong things.

Mad at strangers in the grocery store—
their carts, their smiles, their whole lives.

Mad.
Mad.
Mad.

I'm mad at Michael.
Mad when he holds it together
while I'm breaking.
Mad when he breaks
when I need him to hold it together.
Mad when he breathes too loud.
Mad when he's too quiet.

I know he's grieving too.
But sometimes I need to blame someone.
And he's the safest target.

Then I hate myself for that, too.

But mostly?

I'm mad at me.

Mad at my body for not protecting Parker.
Mad at my instincts for not screaming louder, sooner.

I know it's not fair.
I know that's not how cancer works.
Still—I blame me.

And the worst part?

There's no one to blame.

But I still want someone to hurt the way I do.

***

One afternoon, Parker was deep in a chemo nap.
Michael rubbed his back, gentle and steady.

I left the room—
lungs too tight,
heart too loud.
Running outside,
begging the city noise to drown me.

And I saw them.
A father and daughter.
Maybe five.
She tugged his sleeve,
showing him a sticker, waiting for his eyes.
He didn't even look up. Kept scrolling.

I almost lost it.

Wanted to walk over and scream:
Do you have any idea how lucky you are?
Look at her. *Just look.*

I didn't, of course.
Kept moving.

But I carried it.

That fury. That disbelief. That ache.

That man had no idea what he was holding.

The first belly-laugh—
my fake sneeze,
the funniest thing he'd ever heard.

Tiny feet,
after school, straight into me.

Counting to twenty—
pride spilling,
that grin.

Puzzle conquered—
small hands holding the win.

I wanted to hurl it into his chest—
laughs, milestones, every fragile moment—
until he saw what I see.

Until he knew what it costs
to beg for one more ordinary day.

Until he felt, for one second,
the fire that's burning me alive.

***

There are days I want to scream until I pass out.

Tear the room apart so something—
anything—
looks as wrecked as I feel.

Moments—dark, fast, sharp—
where I don't recognize myself.

The rage curdles into shame.

I swallow it.
I smile.
I lie.

Rage is a language I never meant to learn.
But now I'm fluent.

And honestly?
It's easier than hope.
Less fragile. Less breakable.

Sometimes, rage is what keeps you upright—
a recognition that something is deeply, violently wrong.

Proof that in the ruin, you're still here.

CHAPTER 15

I am no longer Parker's lifeline—
just the one holding the line.

Nothing I do can stop what's inside him.
I'm just a witness.

Before, I was the medicine.
Held him through fevers that drenched us both.
Rocked him while my own body ached.
Sang with no voice left.
Ate the scraps he wouldn't finish.
Slept upright, half-conscious—
drool and sweat,
our signature scent: *Making It Through the Night.*

It always worked.
He got sick.
I got sicker.
We healed.
The exhaustion felt earned.
My love made him better.

Then—fever meant Tylenol.
Now—blood cultures.
Pack the bag. Call the team.
Stand under fluorescent lights

while they hesitate before touching his port.

Vomiting isn't a symptom.
It's the side effect of the side effect.

Lips cracked, trembling.
I touch his arm.
He pulls away.

I eat in the bathroom.
Fan on.
Door shut.
Salad over the sink
so the smell doesn't make him retch.

No "almost over."
We are nowhere near over.

Tucked into the hospital bed.
Hip twisted. Neck stiff.
Frozen—don't tug a line,
trip a wire, wake the room.

My skin touching his,
and still my body feels useless—
like proximity should mean power,
but all I have is presence.

Michael and I make cafeteria runs for the motion, not the food.
When food doesn't work, I drink.

I have my father's blood.

Tired that lives
in my bones
my teeth
my bloodstream.

My body is a home for grief now.
A shut-down system that keeps going because it has to.
I wear what stretches, what hides.
Mourning clothes on house arrest.

The actress, the artist—
buried under pharmacy runs and feeding pump resets.
My career is a past life.

I love Parker with everything I have.
And still—I miss the woman who had more to give.

I think of her often.

Staying up late with Michael—
trying new wines,
discovering new shows,
finding reasons to stay awake in a quiet house.

She felt whole.

Will I ever come back?
Or is this it?
Is grief my personality now?
Do I get a punch card?

Please don't die.

I thought I knew hard.
I forget the old hard.
It feels like another life—
one I'd give anything to return to.

Hard isn't just what it asks of him—
it's what it takes from me.
The right to fix it.
To trade places.
To make it better with a washcloth
and a whispered song.

Now all I can do is watch.
Hold.
Show up.
Even when I'm falling apart.

So I contort into the bed again.
Worthless hands—
except for the one on his back,
counting the breaths
he doesn't know I'm counting.

Because he still needs me to be the medicine—
even when I can't heal a thing.

CHAPTER 16

Fingertips grazing his head—
sparse wisps under my palm,
the faint warmth of him.

It slips in from the shadows.
Arrives in the tender moments—
sacred moments.

A laugh.
A song he used to love.

Light—
Ache.

Hold tighter.
Don't think it.
Don't say it.

***

If he dies—
The house goes still.
Air stale.
Toothbrush by the sink.
Socks balled in the drawer.

Hot Wheels in a crooked line on the floor.

If he lives—
He fights to be himself.
Even now.
Especially now.

If he dies—
who am I then?
Drink more.
Eat less.
Never leave the bed.
Dissolve.
Diminish.

If he lives—
playground; slide hot from the sun.
"I had cancer. The special medicine takes away my sick.
They take my blood because the blood has answers."

If he dies—
I won't be whole.
I won't survive.

If he lives—
smile when they say,
"He looks amazing."
Jaw clenched.
"Thanks, I grew him myself."

If he dies—
stop breathing.

If he lives—
never exhale.

Wait for the day it feels safe—
maybe it comes.

Maybe it doesn't.

I hold you.
Tighter.
Breathe with you.

Please stay.

CHAPTER 17

We met in the South Wing playroom.
Early. Quiet.
Toys already wiped down.

Our kids pressed play dough at a tiny table.
No words.
Just passing tools—
like they knew that's how connection works here.

Her daughter still had hair.
A reminder of the world outside these walls.
A world where children grow
without having to fight for it.

She looked like someone
who belonged somewhere else—
who'd escaped, then come back.

The mom sat close.
Hand on her daughter's leg.
Fixed there.
As if letting go
means something terrible happens.

I asked first.
"What are you navigating?"

She didn't look at me.
Watched the dough.

"She relapsed."

The air shifted—
that silence when someone's world splits open,
and yours remembers.

Relapse.
The worst word.

Not cancer again—
cancer again after you already survived it once.

They'd been out. Made plans. Imagined life.

Then—persistent pain.
Bloodwork.
Scans.
Back in.

Her voice carried it—
insomnia,
caffeine,
hope stretched thin.

I told her about Parker.
The meds.
The side effects.
The way he looks at me
like I'm part of the hurt.

She didn't waver. She knew.

Two moms.
Side by side.
Pretending stillness,
while everything inside us unraveled.

That's what we do.
Until we can't.
And even then—
we keep going.
We don't break the tether.

Back in the room,
Parker slept—
small, tangled,
IV cords like extra limbs.

I kissed his cheek.
Stayed there.

Grateful he was sleeping.
Grateful for him.
Grateful I'm not alone.

CHAPTER 18

I don't remember the first time I said it.
Maybe in the ER hallway.
Maybe in the dark, curled beside him,
when I realized he smelled like sickness—
metallic, faintly sour.

Already slipping.

But once it started,
it never stopped.

Please don't die.

It became my breath.
My heartbeat.

The rhythm
under every syringe push,
every pump beep,
every soft-footed doctor
with bad news in their eyes.

Sometimes I whisper it
into his skin
while he sleeps—
please—

like I'm trying to bargain with his cells.

As if they might listen
if I'm gentle enough.

CHAPTER 19

People talk about survival like it's an ending.
A clean scan.
A bell rung.
A banner: *You made it.*

Trust me—we're counting the days.
Counting down to ring that fucking bell.
To leave that place behind,
clapped out by the same hands that held us together.

But survival isn't the finish line.
It's the now.
Here, in the thick of it.

Even when he lives—
nothing ends.

There's still the medicine.
The monitoring.
The body that remembers.
The grief that taps on the walls at night.

And there's him.
More him than ever.

***

What he carries now isn't just trauma.
It's wisdom.

He teaches us what it means to live.
Resilience isn't teeth-gritting optimism.

It's curiosity.
It's stubborn wonder.
It's the refusal to stop being yourself—
even when the world tries to erase you.

We used to build scaffolding.
Now we build space—
for Parker to become whoever he is.

Without fear.
Without apology.

When he lives,
we are not the same.
We are better.
Not because we needed a lesson.
Not because cancer is a gift.

But because Parker—
even stripped down, cut open, poisoned—
refused to disappear.

He stayed Parker.

And in doing so—
he taught us how to stay ourselves too.

***

Some days,
I want to carve it into walls.
Tattoo it across my palms.

Scream it into the sky
until it screams back:
He won't.

But no one can promise that.
Not even the ones who try.

So I say it again.
And again.
As if repetition could be protection.

Because that's all I can do.

All I have left.
All that matters.

Even on good days—
rare stretches of calm,
bursts of normalcy—
when he begs to make slime,
when he belts Rob Zombie
from his car seat,
when he lists, with absurd precision,
which dinosaurs are carnivores.

Please don't die.

Not because
I believe he will.

But because loving him
means never stopping—
not the hoping,
not the prayer.

Not ever.

CHAPTER 20

He's in the backyard.
Bug hunting.
Chasing dandelion fragments—
soft explosions drifting just out of reach.

We're still here.
Months into a two-year protocol.
"It'll get easier, right?"

Hell if I know.

Pain just shape-shifts.

Parker's still fighting.
Still dancing.
Still asking questions that split me open.

The three of us, clinging to what's left,
refusing to let go.

I'm still mothering in the blur.
Folding around him—
like my body could keep the world out.

Living one minute,
one blood count,

one scan at a time.

Joy in one breath.
Grief in the next.

***

Our village found us here—
under hospital light,
in the wreckage.

Over a thousand donors.
Names I know.
Names I don't.
People I haven't spoken to in years.
People I've never met.

All saying: *We've got you.*

Friends making the house breathe again.
Family dropping everything.
Takeout cards.
The check gone before we could reach for it.
Gifts for Parker.
Venmo: *whatever you need.*
Texts: *I'm here.*

The village that comes
when your house is burning—and stays.
Shattered.
Scorched.
Undone.

But if I stand still,
I can see the beauty in the ashes.

When my arms shake from holding Parker up—
I feel arms beneath mine.
Holding us both.

The tether:
my father's hand.
My mother's absence—
the knot.
Me, bound
to my son.

***

People ask why I wrote this.
Not to solve it.
Not to explain.

But to give the pain a place to live
while it still moves through us—
before time softens it,
before memory
makes it something else.

A place to set it down.
To see it whole.
To say: *This happened.*

Not to say we survived—

but to say we existed.
Loved through it.
Stayed.

There's no road back.
Only forward.
Not because we want to.
Because there's no other way.

We carry it all.
For him.

For Parker.

Toweling him dry—
backyard dirt rinsed away,
water clinging to skin,
his weight soft in my arms.

Curled around him,
cheek wet against mine.

Please
don't—
let
go.

Please—

until I can't tell
which words are his
and which have been living in me all along.

Thank you for holding these words close—for seeing Parker, for seeing us, and for daring to journey *with* us through the dark.

May the truths within these pages—imperfect and unresolved— illuminate the tangled, unrelenting landscape of illness, or remind you that you are not alone in the fierce and tender work of parenting through cancer.

However this story found you, may it leave you with this: love—in all its messy forms—is enough to hold us upright, even in our darkest moments.

With gratitude,
Amber Sweet-Davis